968.06   Watson, R   L
Wa
        South Africa in
        pictures

17390

Visual Geography Series®

SOUTH AFRICA

...in Pictures

Prepared by
R. L. Watson

Lerner Publications Company
Minneapolis

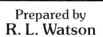

17390

Independent Picture Service

Fishermen at Hout Bay mend their nets.

This is an all-new edition of the Visual Geography
Series. Previous editions have been published by
Sterling Publishing Company, New York City, and
some of the original textual information has been retained. New photographs, maps, charts, captions, and
updated information have been added. The text has
been entirely reset in 10/12 Century Textbook.

LIBRARY OF CONGRESS CATALOGING-IN-PUBLICATION DATA

Watson, R. L. (Richard Lyness), 1945–
    South Africa in pictures / prepared by R. L. Watson.
    p.   cm.—(Visual geography series)
    Rev. ed. of: South Africa in pictures / prepared by Peter
English.
    Includes index.
    Summary: Introduces the geography, history, govern-
ment, economy, people and culture of the troubled
Republic of South Africa.
    ISBN 0-8225-1835-X (lib. bdg.)
    1. South Africa. [1. South Africa.] I. English, Peter.
South Africa in pictures.   II. Title.   III. Series: Visual
geography series (Minneapolis, Minn.)
DT779.9.W37 1988
968.06—dc19   87–27039
                                                  CIP
                                                  AC

International Standard Book Number: 0-8225-1835-X
Library of Congress Card Catalog Number: 87-27039

VISUAL GEOGRAPHY SERIES®

Publisher
Harry Jonas Lerner
Associate Publisher
Nancy M. Campbell
Senior Editor
Mary M. Rodgers
Editor
Gretchen Bratvold
Illustrations Editor
Karen A. Sirvaitis
Consultants/Contributors
Thomas O'Toole
R. L. Watson
Sandra K. Davis
Designer
Jim Simondet
Cartographer
Carol F. Barrett
Indexer
Sylvia Timian
Production Manager
Richard J. Hannah

Independent Picture Service

Cattle graze in the Nqutu district of the KwaZulu homeland.

Acknowledgments

Title page photo courtesy of SATOUR.

Elevation contours adapted from *The Times Atlas of
the World*, seventh comprehensive edition (New York:
Times Books, 1985).

The protea, with its thistlelike buds, is the national flower of the Republic of South Africa.

Courtesy of SATOUR

Contents

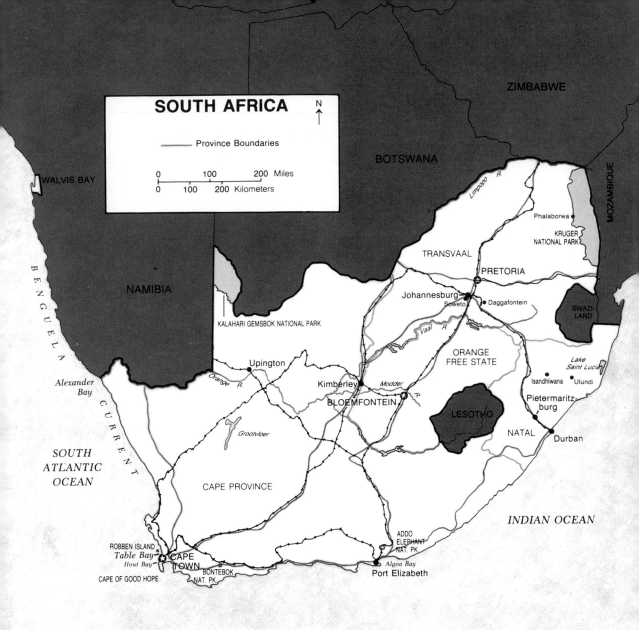

SOUTH AFRICA

N ↑

—— Province Boundaries

| 0 | 100 | 200 Miles |
| 0 | 100 | 200 Kilometers |

ZIMBABWE

BOTSWANA

WALVIS BAY

B E N G U E L A

NAMIBIA

Alexander Bay

C U R R E N T

SOUTH ATLANTIC OCEAN

KALAHARI GEMSBOK NATIONAL PARK

Upington

Orange R.

Kimberley

Modder R.

BLOEMFONTEIN

Grootvloer

CAPE PROVINCE

Limpopo R.

TRANSVAAL

PRETORIA

Johannesburg
Soweto • Daggafontein

Vaal R.

ORANGE FREE STATE

LESOTHO

Phalaborwa •
KRUGER NATIONAL PARK

MOZAMBIQUE

SWAZI-LAND

Lake Saint Lucia

Isandhlwana • Ulundi

Pietermaritz-burg

NATAL

Durban

INDIAN OCEAN

ADDO ELEPHANT NAT. PK.

ROBBEN ISLAND
Table Bay
Hout Bay
CAPE TOWN
CAPE OF GOOD HOPE
BONTEBOK NAT. PK.

Algoa Bay
Port Elizabeth

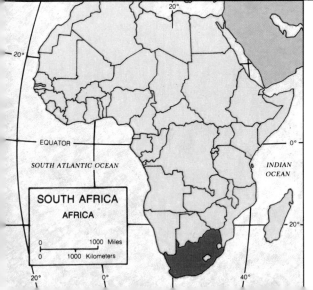

20°

20°

EQUATOR

SOUTH ATLANTIC OCEAN

INDIAN OCEAN

0°

20°

SOUTH AFRICA
AFRICA

| 0 | 1000 Miles |
| 0 | 1000 Kilometers |

20°   0°   40°

METRIC CONVERSION CHART
To Find Approximate Equivalents

WHEN YOU KNOW:	MULTIPLY BY:	TO FIND:
AREA		
acres	0.41	hectares
square miles	2.59	square kilometers
CAPACITY		
gallons	3.79	liters
LENGTH		
feet	30.48	centimeters
yards	0.91	meters
miles	1.61	kilometers
MASS (weight)		
pounds	0.45	kilograms
tons	0.91	metric tons
VOLUME		
cubic yards	0.77	cubic meters
TEMPERATURE		
degrees Fahrenheit	0.56 (*after* subtracting 32)	degrees Celsius

Although aspects of apartheid—the South African policy of racial separateness—have been reformed, some public accommodations are still segregated.

Introduction

A visitor to South Africa who has not read news headlines might see only a modern industrial society that offers many pleasures. The climate is mild, and large cities—such as Cape Town and Johannesburg—welcome the newcomer. Mountains, beaches, deserts, lush green countryside, and spectacular game parks abound.

But the contrasts to the pleasant scenes are striking. Most rural whites are Afrikaners who live in spacious, well-kept houses either on farms or in country villages. Most rural blacks live in the homelands—acreages set aside for blacks by the white-controlled government—or on farms owned by whites, where the blacks are laborers.

For 40 years, a minority white population has used its political power to segregate itself from those who are not white through a system called apartheid (the Afrikaans word for apartness). "Whites Only" signs are visible on beaches and in waiting rooms, and spray-painted anti-apartheid slogans color the walls of buildings in major cities. Furthermore, a noticeable tension exists between blacks, who continue to agitate for reform, and the police, who enforce the status quo.

In 1989 the population of South Africa was over 35 million. For decades, the government has divided South Africans into four main groups—whites, Coloureds, Asians, and blacks. The politically dominant whites number about 16 percent, of which about 40 percent are those whose principal language is English. Sixty percent of the whites speak Afrikaans, a language derived from Dutch.

The second group, called Coloureds, are people of mixed ancestry. They form about 10 percent of the population. About

The traditional dwelling among South Africa's black ethnic groups is a kraal, a compound that includes a round structure with a grass-covered roof.

3 percent are Asians, most of whom are East Indians. By far the largest group is the blacks, who, at times, also have been called Bantu, natives, or Africans. They number approximately 20 million, and are made up of several ethnic groups, including the Zulu, Tswana, Sotho, and Xhosa.

The policy of apartheid has created national tensions unlike those of any other country on the African continent. Few places in the world have as lively a variety of cultures; few have as many natural resources; few have a society that is as controversial.

Farmhouses owned by white Afrikaners are spacious and sturdy, with a distinctly Dutch architectural flavor in the curved gables above the front door.

Cape Point, near the southernmost tip of the African continent, is the site of a nature reserve where rare flowers grow and where endangered animals live and breed in safety.

1) The Land

The Republic of South Africa lies at the southern tip of the African continent. The nation shares its northwestern border with Namibia (called South-West Africa by the South African government). To the north are Botswana and Zimbabwe; to the northeast are Mozambique and Swaziland. The Indian Ocean washes against South Africa's eastern shore, and the South Atlantic Ocean forms the nation's western border. The waters of the two oceans merge at the Cape of Good Hope, located at the southernmost tip of the entire continent.

The Republic of South Africa proper consists of four provinces: Cape Province, Natal, the Transvaal, and the Orange Free State, which together cover a total area of 472,359 square miles. The republic also administers South-West Africa (recognized as independent Namibia by the United Nations), which has an area of 318,099 square miles.

In 1948 South Africa claimed ownership of two small islands, Prince Edward and Marion, which lie about 1,200 miles southeast of Cape Town. The small territory of Walvis Bay, on the coast of Namibia, is an integral part of the Republic of South Africa's economy, with important fishing and shipping facilities. The independent kingdom of Lesotho, formerly the British protectorate of Basutoland, is completely surrounded by South African territory.

Topography

Massive in size, South Africa is slightly larger in area than the states of California, Arizona, Utah, and Nevada combined. Four regions—the plateaus, or velds (the Afrikaans word for grassy plains); the Great Escarpment and other highlands; the coastal regions; and the desert areas —characterize South Africa's topography.

The landscape is dominated by the plateaus, which extend from the Transvaal, across the Orange Free State, and through the northern section of Cape Province. Within the plateaus, several subdivisions are noticeable. The largest area is the High Veld, a region of rolling grasslands bordered by the Witwatersrand ridge, which lies in the southern Transvaal and is a watershed, or dividing point, for several of

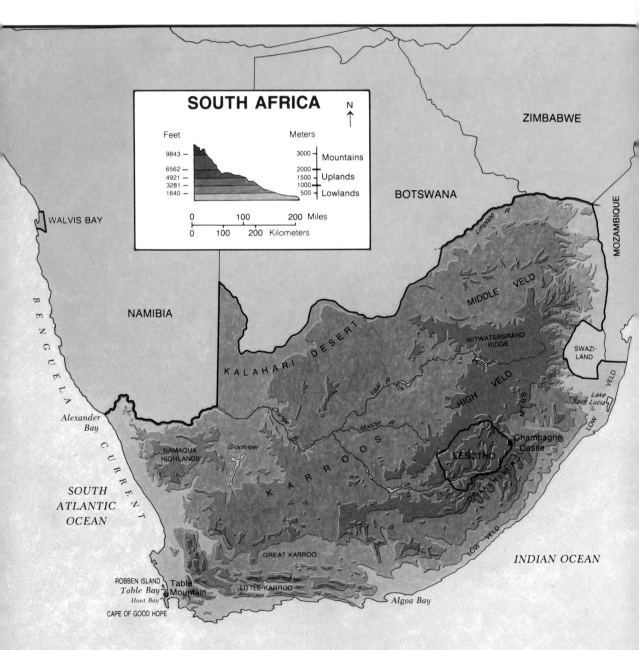

SOUTH AFRICA

Photo by Amandus Schneider

The landscape of the Transvaal includes a section of the High Veld, as well as lower plateaus that are watered by small rivers.

South Africa's rivers. The High Veld is famous for its vast gold deposits. The Middle Veld—north of the Witwatersrand—consists of dry grasslands, beyond which is the Limpopo River Valley.

Several mountain ranges form a rocky wall along the eastern and southern edges of the plateaus and are collectively called the Great Escarpment. The escarpment extends in an almost unbroken chain from northern Zimbabwe southward, skirting the southern edge of the African continent. Within the escarpment are the Drakensburg Mountains to the northeast. The Namaqua Highlands are found in the northwest.

The highest point in South Africa—Champagne Castle (11,073 feet above sea level)—is on the border between South Africa and Lesotho. Two elevated plains, the Little Karroo and the Great Karroo, lie among the mountains along the southwestern plateau edge. Few plants grow on the dry mountains, but farms thrive in the valleys and the lowlands.

Courtesy of R. L. Watson

Scrub vegetation characterizes many regions of South Africa, where, in general, rainfall is not plentiful.

9

Located in Natal and Cape Province, the Drakensburg Mountains extend through South Africa's eastern regions.

Rocky foothills stretching down from the escarpment, together with slopes leading up from the coast, form the Low Veld, much of which was shaped by erosion. A narrow coastal strip rises from the Atlantic and Indian oceans to an average height of 500 to 600 feet. This strip varies in width from over 30 miles in the northeast to as little as 3 miles in the south.

South Africa's west coast is a desert, although during most of the year a small amount of rain falls along the southwestern coast. The Kalahari Desert occupies parts of northern Cape Province along the Middle Veld and stretches into Botswana and Namibia. Around the Cape of Good Hope and northeast of Port Elizabeth, coastal areas can be hot and humid.

The Homelands

A glance at most maps will reveal dozens of small land units scattered over much of eastern South Africa. These are the homelands, once called Bantustans. Until recently, they were a primary feature of apartheid —the white-controlled government's plan for the separate development of South Africa's white and nonwhite populations. Together, the land fragments form 10 homelands, and each eventually was supposed to receive independence from South Africa. Blacks would be allowed to live in the rest of South Africa only if they held jobs outside the homelands.

In order to implement its homelands policy, the government removed blacks from white areas if they were not employed there. Many blacks lived all their lives in areas that were suddenly restricted to whites. Families were uprooted and sometimes were separated. More than 232,000 blacks were forcibly resettled from 1968 to 1972, and removals continued into the 1980s.

By 1987 four homelands—Transkei, Bophuthatswana, Ciskei, and Venda—had accepted independence. The remaining six, however, have refused it, arguing that their share of South Africa's land and resources is inadequate. No other nation in the world recognizes the independence of the homelands.

Rivers and Lakes

South Africa has only three large rivers— the Orange, the Vaal, and the Limpopo.

Independent Picture Service

At Upington in northern Cape Province, the Orange River flows near fertile fields.

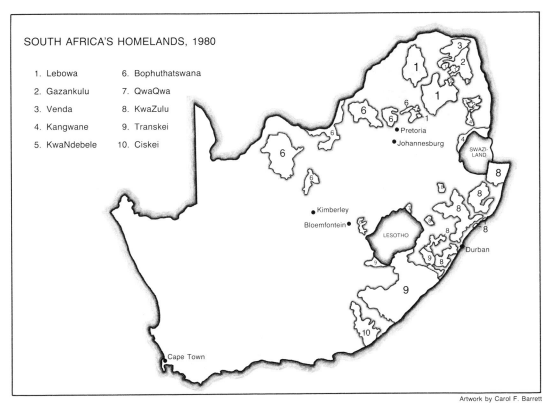

SOUTH AFRICA'S HOMELANDS, 1980

1. Lebowa
2. Gazankulu
3. Venda
4. Kangwane
5. KwaNdebele
6. Bophuthatswana
7. QwaQwa
8. KwaZulu
9. Transkei
10. Ciskei

Artwork by Carol F. Barrett

Established by the South African government, the 10 African homelands consist of many small land fragments located throughout the country. Each homeland has been offered independent status, but only four—Transkei, Ciskei, Venda, and Bophuthatswana—have accepted it. Map taken from *South Africa, A County Study,* 1980.

The 1,300-mile-long Orange River—the most extensive of South Africa's waterways—flows west from its source in Lesotho to the Atlantic Ocean at Alexander Bay. Dammed at many places along its course to supply hydroelectric power, the Orange waters much of Cape Province.

A tributary of the Orange, the Vaal, begins in the southeastern Transvaal and forms the boundary between that province and the Orange Free State. Eventually, the Vaal flows west to join the Orange River in the northern reaches of Cape Province.

The Limpopo has its source near Johannesburg. Its 1,100-mile-long course flows north and then northeast to form South Africa's border with Zimbabwe. The river then cuts south through Mozambique to reach the Indian Ocean.

The mountains that surround the coastal region, as well as sandbars and inadequate rainfall to feed the rivers, combine to prevent ships from sailing more than a few miles inland from the shore. In general, South Africa's rivers are dry during much of the year. Moreover, very few freshwater lakes exist in South Africa; most so-called lakes are really lagoons. Marshy areas—called vleis or pans—form in low places during the rainy season but contain great concentrations of salt. Some of these saltwater bodies are quite large—Grootvloer is 39 miles long and 24 miles wide.

Natural Resources

Enormous mineral deposits—particularly of gold and diamonds—account for a great part of the wealth of South Africa. The nation produces almost two-thirds of the world's gold and over one-quarter of its gem diamonds. The Transvaal and the Orange Free State contain the principal gold fields, as well as substantial deposits of asbestos, chromium (from which chrome is made), coal, iron, platinum, tin, and uranium (used to produce nuclear energy). Indeed, South Africa contains

Courtesy of SATOUR

Lake Saint Lucia on the eastern coast of Natal province is an inlet of the Indian Ocean.

Courtesy of SATOUR

This big hole at Kimberley owes its existence to a huge diamond mine that was established there. Now closed, the mine produced nearly 15 million carats (three tons) of diamonds in its time.

The skyline of Johannesburg forms a backdrop for the gold mine dumps located just outside of the city.

nearly every mineral necessary for industry except oil. In contrast, little of its land receives enough rainfall to make farming profitable or easy.

Climate

Although temperatures in South Africa vary greatly with altitude, much of the country enjoys a mild, sunny climate most of the year. In Durban, a low-lying city on the northeastern coast, temperatures in January—during the Southern Hemisphere's summer—stand at about 75° F. Johannesburg, roughly in the center of the country, reaches averages of 66° F in the same month. Under the influence of cool ocean breezes, Cape Town's temperature stays at about 68° F in January.

Only about one-third of the land receives more than the minimum—25 inches—of rain a year needed to raise crops. The eastern half of the republic usually has more rain than the western. This general dryness makes much of the land suitable only for grazing.

13

Flora and Fauna

Despite its relatively arid climate, South Africa has a wealth of plants and animals. Aardvarks, cheetahs, leopards, jackals, lions, elephants, rhinoceroses, wild buffalo, hippopotamuses, and many varieties of antelope are still found in isolated parts of the country. In South Africa's game parks, many of the animals that once roamed freely still live in natural surroundings.

The variety of both smaller animals and plants is so great that all have not been fully identified yet. The ostrich is among the most spectacular of the 900 kinds of native birds, and 200 species of snakes inhabit the land. The number of insect varieties is estimated at 40,000; and about 1,000 kinds of fish are found in South African waters.

Rainfall—or lack of it—determines the variety of much of South Africa's flora. In the eastern Low Veld, for example, where

Courtesy of SATOUR

A thirsty lioness warily drinks from a stream in one of South Africa's many protected wildlife areas.

rainfall is heaviest, tropical palm trees thrive. Also in this area are forests of yellowwood, ironwood, and cedar. Since much of South Africa is grassland, it is not surprising that about 350 different kinds of heath (low shrubs that grow in flat, open spaces) thrive in areas such as Cape Province. In addition, more than 500 species of grasses are found throughout the country. Where rainfall is light, vegetation is poor, and, in some areas of the karroos, only dry scrub can survive.

South Africa has set aside large acreages to help preserve its wildlife. Addo Elephant National Park is in southern Cape Province, and Bontebok National Park is a habitat for the last surviving herd of bontebok antelope. Kalahari Gemsbok National Park lies in the southwestern Kalahari Desert, and Kruger National Park contains almost every South African animal in its natural habitat.

Courtesy of SATOUR

The aloe plant, whose bitter juice has medicinal properties, is a wildflower native to South Africa.

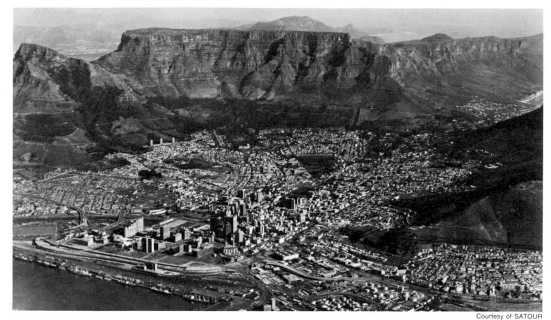

Cape Town lies at the foot of Table Mountain in a natural harbor off Table Bay. As both a major seaport and capital city, Cape Town has highly developed urban facilities.

Capital Cities

When Cape Colony, Natal, the Transvaal, and the Orange Free State united into the Union of South Africa in 1910, the large cities of the main provinces took their part in the national government. Thus, the Republic of South Africa has three capital cities, each of which is the site of a particular governmental function.

Founded in 1652 by Jan van Riebeeck, Cape Town (metropolitan population 1.4 million) ranks as one of the most beautiful of the world's seaports. Indeed, as well as being the republic's second largest city and the legislative capital, Cape Town is among the nation's chief ports, lying along the sea routes between Europe and eastern Asia. In a green and pleasant setting of gardens and trees, the city reflects the cultural influences of Europe, Asia, and Africa.

Pretoria (metropolitan population 585,400), South Africa's fourth largest city, is the administrative capital of the republic and one of the loveliest of the

Pretoria's Voortrekker Monument commemorates the Great Trek of Boer farmers in the 1830s.

inland cities. It was founded in 1855 as a religious and administrative seat by Marthinus Pretorius, the son of the leader of the Voortrekkers (pioneers). Situated in the folds of successive ranges of hills, it has a sunny climate. In the spring, purple jacarandas bloom along the streets, in the gardens of the Union Buildings, and at the foot of the Voortrekker Monument.

The judicial capital, Bloemfontein (metropolitan population 198,340), hosts the appeals division of the judical branch. Meaning "fountain of flowers" in Afrikaans, Bloemfontein was founded by Afrikaners in 1846 at a spot along a tributary of the Modder River. In the 1980s more Africans than Afrikaners worked in the city, which also serves as a farming and marketing hub.

Other Urban Centers

South Africa's cities, compared to those of Europe and the East, are young. Modern and well-planned, the cities are home to about one-third of South Africa's entire population.

The City Hall in Durban, South Africa's chief port, is a bright landmark on the city's evening skyline.

Johannesburg is South Africa's largest city and leading industrial center. In addition to gold mines, the city features factories that produce chemicals, textiles, and leather goods.

South Africa's townships have developed on the outskirts of the country's large cities. The black workers who live in these sprawling shantytowns are employed in the cities but are prohibited by law from living in urban areas.

South Africa's largest city, Johannesburg (metropolitan population 1.7 million), was founded in 1886 after a huge lode of gold was discovered in the heart of the Witwatersrand area. Forty percent of the city's population is employed by the gold mines. The city is also the nation's financial and industrial center, producing diamonds, machinery, textiles, furniture, and chemicals in large quantities.

Durban (metropolitan population 960,800), the third largest city, is a principal port of the republic. Like Cape Town, it has a diverse population, and its city streets reflect its large East Indian population. Founded in 1834 on a splendid harbor on the Indian Ocean, Durban has developed into a major transportation center, as well as an important resort city.

Situated on Algoa Bay, Port Elizabeth (metropolitan population 585,400), is the third largest port after Cape Town and Durban. The city was founded in 1820 when the first British settlers landed there. Today Port Elizabeth is one of South Africa's principal industrial hubs, producing automobiles and rubber and handling the region's exports of citrus fruits and mineral ores.

Townships

Because the policy of apartheid aims to separate whites from nonwhites, African townships, where black workers live, are very different from attractive cities. Many townships and temporary settlements are no more than large slums where residents live in cramped, substandard housing that lacks plumbing and electricity.

Soweto, outside Johannesburg, for example, has more than 1.5 million people, making it one of the largest African urban areas on the entire continent. Crossroads, a squatter settlement near Cape Town, has more than 20,000 residents.

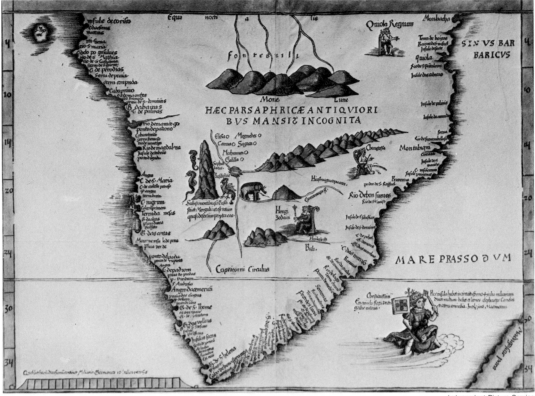

Portuguese explorers rounded the tip of the African continent in the fifteenth century. Maps based on their findings included little information about the interior, which was rarely penetrated by the early Europeans.

2) History and Government

Ancestors of humans lived in the area now called South Africa as long as two million years ago. But South Africa's known history begins with the San (called Bushmen by the Europeans) and the Khoikhoi (later dubbed Hottentots). These two groups were firmly established in eastern and western South Africa by A.D. 1500.

Hunters of the abundant game in the region and gatherers of wild vegetation, these peoples may have been a single ethnic group at one time. (They are sometimes jointly referred to as the Khoisan.)

But for reasons that may be related to their means of making a living, they split into separate communities many generations before the Europeans arrived. The San continued to hunt, gather, and live a nomadic life in small groupings. The Khoikhoi became herders of cattle and formed large political units.

Meanwhile, before A.D. 100, Bantu-speaking peoples began a slow, southward migration from central Africa into what is now the eastern Transvaal region. By 1500 one of these groups had occupied large sections of modern Natal and eastern Cape Province. These peoples spoke languages from which modern Zulu, Xhosa, and Swazi descend. Indeed, journals of sixteenth-century European adventurers noted the existence of substantial Bantu-speaking populations along the Natal coast. Another Bantu-speaking group, the Sotho, spread west and southwest from the eastern ransvaal. These peoples formed kingdoms and supported themselves by herding livestock and by growing a few agricultural crops, mostly cereal grains.

The Coming of the Europeans

In the late fifteenth century, navigators of European trading nations, such as Portugal, were searching for ocean routes to the

Independent Picture Service

The Portuguese explorer Bartolomeu Dias was the first European to touch the shores of South Africa. He reached Algoa Bay in 1488 and named the landing point, where he erected a cross, Cabo da Bôa Esperança ("Cape of Good Hope").

Courtesy of SATOUR

While the Portuguese explored the coastal regions, the San — a well-established ethnic community that was living in eastern and western parts of southern Africa — continued to hunt and gather. Modern-day descendants of this early people pursue a similar existence in the Kalahari Desert.

rich spice markets of the East. A Portuguese captain named Bartolomeu Dias visited the Cape of Good Hope in 1488, and Vasco da Gama stopped there on his way to India in 1497. Their explorations brought South Africa's inhabitants in contact with Europeans for the first time. Portuguese ships began to use these new sea-lanes almost immediately. The Europeans eased the problem of resupplying their vessels en route to the East by establishing outposts along the coasts of the Atlantic and Indian oceans.

Portugal's power waned by the end of the sixteenth century, and English and Dutch trading vessels competed for control of the valuable spice route. Although the English occasionally stopped at the Cape of Good Hope, the first Europeans to settle there were Dutch. In 1651 the Dutch East India Company sent Jan van Riebeeck to establish a settlement. The site would provide fresh food and water for ships bound for Dutch colonies in the East Indies. Riebeeck and his settlers arrived at Table Bay near the Cape in 1652.

The Dutch East India Company sent surgeon Jan van Riebeeck to South Africa in 1651.

Dutch Settlement

The Dutch had not intended to establish a permanent colony at the Cape. But the settlers saw a chance to prosper by farming on their own and expanded farther inland, where they encountered the San and the Khoikhoi. Most of these African peoples regarded all livestock—including Dutch cattle—as wild game and took or killed the animals tamed by the Dutch. As a result, the Dutch declared war on the Khoikhoi and easily defeated them, taking over valuable pastureland in the process.

Beginning in the late seventeenth century, German, French, and more Dutch settlers began to arrive at the Cape, attracted by offers of free farmland. More wars with the Khoikhoi erupted as a result of Dutch efforts to provide the promised acreages to the newcomers. The Khoikhoi finally began to diminish because of Dutch raids and new diseases (such as smallpox) introduced by the Europeans, and because they sold too many of their cattle. These problems destroyed their traditional way of life, and many surviving Khoikhoi had to work as servants for the Dutch in order to make a living.

The Dutch also attempted to possess the lands of the San. As skilled hunters, however, the San were able to put up a strong resistance, using poison-tipped arrows to fell many Dutch sharp-shooters. As a result, the Dutch developed a strong desire to rid the colony of the San and slaughtered many of them on sight. Surviving members of the San retreated to uninviting lands, such as the Kalahari Desert, where they could still hunt but where the Dutch would not settle. Some of those who were captured were put to work as slaves on Dutch farms.

Slaves from other parts of Africa, the East Indies, and southeast Asia began to be imported in the late 1650s to work on the large farms and cattle ranches that the settlers had established. By 1808 the Cape was a struggling colony of about 20,000 people, in which a minority of whites dom-

Slaves from southeastern Asia, particularly from Indonesia, began to arrive in South Africa in the 1650s. Many were followers of the Islamic religion, and their descendants built mosques (Islamic places of worship) in which to practice the faith of their ancestors.

Courtesy of R. L. Watson

inated enslaved populations. Because few European women immigrated to the Cape, many Dutch men had children by Khoikhoi and slave women. These children helped to form the basis of the Cape's Coloured population, which now includes the only trace of the original Khoikhoi people.

Black African Kingdoms

By the mid-eighteenth century the southernmost of the Nguni-speaking migrants, the Xhosa, encountered the Dutch. During the next 100 years, relations between the Xhosa and the whites were marked by both cooperative trading and cattle raiding. By 1857, however, the Xhosa had lost their land and independent way of life to Dutch expansion.

Competition among increasing numbers of blacks for good farmland and grazing land resulted in the emergence of several powerful, well-organized African kingdoms to protect their holdings. The most important of these was the Zulu Empire, led by its warrior-founder Shaka. Using modern ideas—such as standing armies and improved weaponry—Shaka shaped his troops into vigorous fighters. By the time he was assassinated in 1828, Shaka's empire covered an area larger than Great Britain. The rise of a strong, centralized kingdom—with a single language and a disciplined military force—disrupted the peace of southern sections of the continent for more than 100 years.

Between 1818 and the 1830s, the Zulu conquered many of the surrounding African peoples, some of whom fled north. Partly to defend themselves against the aggressive Zulu, small groupings that had existed in central and eastern South Africa

Founder of the Zulu Empire, Shaka emerged as the leader of his people in 1816 and conquered other African groups in much of southern Africa. In 1828 his half-brothers, Mpande and Dingane, judged Shaka to be insane and killed him.

Courtesy of Cape Archives Depot

The son of a Sotho leader, Moshoeshoe united several small groups to form the Sotho nation. By establishing alliances that seesawed between the British and the Boers, the king avoided being taken over until 1868. Thereafter, the British had control of Mshweshwe's territory, which they called Basutoland. The colony became the independent kingdom of Lesotho in 1966.

merged to form large kingdoms. For example, the Sotho became a nation under their skillful king Moshoeshoe, and the Ndebele organized themselves under Mzilikazi, a former warrior in Shaka's armies. These kingdoms became serious opponents of European expansion into the interior of southern Africa.

South Africa Becomes British

During the Napoleonic wars of the early nineteenth century, Great Britain seized the Cape Colony from the Dutch and eventually set up British-style social and political institutions. This event caused great changes in the lives of the white settlers, most of whom were not British but Boers—the Dutch word for farmers.

Seeking to improve the conditions of the slaves and of the remaining members of the Khoikhoi, the British introduced laws to prevent slave owners from mistreating both groups. In addition, the British made it legal for Coloureds to own land and to move freely within the colony—rights the Dutch had never granted them. Most Boers resented the new measures. When more British settlers arrived in the 1820s, many Boers saw their way of life—with its unlimited claim to cheap labor to work their farms—threatened. The last straw was probably the 1834 act of Parliament (a law enacted by the British legislature) that abolished slavery throughout the British Empire, including South Africa.

In response to these new conditions, several thousand Boers, called Voortrekkers, packed their belongings in 1836 and fled the British colony, going northeast in ox wagons. This migration, known as the Great Trek, is a pivotal event in South African history for the white population. The outcome of the Great Trek was the establishment of two independent Boer republics—the South African Republic, or Transvaal (founded in 1852) and the Orange Free State (founded in 1854).

A frieze, or ornamented band, on the Voortrekker Monument shows the pioneering Boers during their Great Trek to northeastern regions of South Africa.

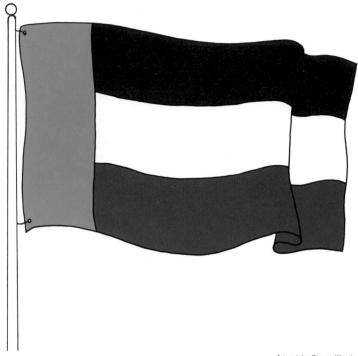

A four-color flag represented the Transvaal while it was an independent state. The banner continues to be the symbol for the region as a province within the Republic of South Africa.

Artwork by Steven Woods

Before these states could be fully established, the Voortrekkers fought African kingdoms, whose land the Boers were absorbing. From the late 1830s until the 1890s, the Voortrekkers battled the Zulu, Sotho, and Ndebele. The ultimate defeat of the Africans was largely due to the Voortrekkers' greater access to European-made firearms.

In addition to African conflicts, the Voortrekkers also repelled repeated British attempts to incorporate these newly established republics into the Cape Colony. After several clashes, the British temporarily gave up trying to overcome the republics. In 1843, however, the British seized Natal, a small Voortrekker republic on the eastern coast.

British Wars Against the Zulu

The aggressive Zulu Empire had declined with the death of Shaka in 1828. His brothers, Dingane and Mpande, ruled after him but lacked Shaka's strongly centralized power structure. The last independent Zulu king, Cetewayo, refused British demands to place a resident commissioner in his realm—an act that would have meant that the Zulu agreed to be governed by the British.

Conflicts with the Europeans resulted in the Zulu War of 1879 against the British. A force of 5,000 Europeans and 8,000 Africans faced 40,000 of Cetewayo's Zulu warriors. The Zulu troops won the first encounter—the Battle of Isandhlwana—despite the superior weaponry of their opponents. Nevertheless, the British finally defeated the Zulu, conquering Cetewayo's capital at Ulundi. The victors officially added Zululand to Britain's South African holdings in 1887.

The Industrialization of South Africa

Rich diamond deposits were discovered near Kimberley in northwestern regions of the Orange Free State in 1867, and gold was found in the Witwatersrand area of

24

the Transvaal in 1884. To the dismay of the Boers, a flood of prospectors, adventurers, and profit-seekers, mostly from the Cape Colony and Great Britain, poured into the two republics. The growth and industrialization caused by the new mining industries brought profound changes in the lives of both black and white South Africans.

The Boers of the Orange Free State and Natal had trekked from the Cape Colony to escape British rule and culture. With the flood of miners entering Boer territory, the British threat returned. The most prominent of the uitlanders (Afrikaans for foreigners) was the British-born financier and Cape Colony politician Cecil John Rhodes. By using aggressive business practices, Rhodes soon monopolized the diamond and gold mining industries in the colony. Firmly convinced that British culture was superior, Rhodes sought to extend it throughout Africa.

A sculpture in Johannesburg commemorates South Africa's mining industry, which began when rich lodes of gold and diamonds were found in the late 1800s.

Zulu fighters—here performing a ceremonial war dance—were a strong force against British and Boer expansion in the nineteenth century.

British Expansion

Rhodes's ambitions included a Cape-to-Cairo rail line that would support the string of British colonies he envisioned in southern and central Africa. In 1889 Rhodes was elected prime minister—the highest colonial official of the Cape Colony—and used his position and wealth to further his goals. The British government backed Rhodes in his efforts to acquire African territories. As a result, the British annexed the land of the Tswana in the north, calling it Bechuanaland (modern Botswana).

The British government also supported the establishment of the British South Africa Company, which took over the lands of the Ndebele and called them Southern Rhodesia (now Zimbabwe). Rhodes's activities soothed British fears about the expansion of German interests in southern Africa. His participation in an illegal and ill-fated attempt to overthrow the Transvaal government, however, forced him to resign as prime minister of the Cape Colony in 1896.

The landscape of South Africa was soon marked by new cities like Johannesburg, by a network of railroads, and by dumps from the mines. The mining boom revolutionized the lives of white and black farmers. The cities needed food, and blacks began to adjust by producing grain for market. Many blacks competed successful-

The aggressive financier and politician Cecil Rhodes encouraged the colonization of South Africa by the British. In a period cartoon he straddles the African continent from Cape Town to Cairo, Egypt — a vast region he believed should be linked by rail to support British expansion and new markets.

Rhodes's ill-fated attempt to take over the Transvaal government ended at the Battle of Doornkop in 1896.

ly with white farmers and had no need to take jobs in the mines. The mines desperately needed labor, and various measures —including discriminatory laws—forced black farmers off their lands and into the new mines and factories to work for low wages.

The Anglo-Boer War

While these changes were occurring, Britain, largely at the urging of Rhodes and the uitlanders, again became interested in dominating the Boer republics. Paul Kruger, the president of the Transvaal, led the movement that resisted the threat to the Boer way of life.

Tensions became so severe that war broke out in 1899. During the war, the British forced both Africans and Boer women and children into concentration camps, while Boer commandos conducted guerrilla warfare. Nearly 28,000 Boers died in the camps—more than the number who died in battle. The Anglo-Boer War embittered British-Boer relations for several generations.

Stretcher-bearers carry the wounded from an ambulance train during the Anglo-Boer War. The casualties came from a field hospital at the Modder River.

The Boers finally surrendered in 1902, and South Africa—from the Cape to the

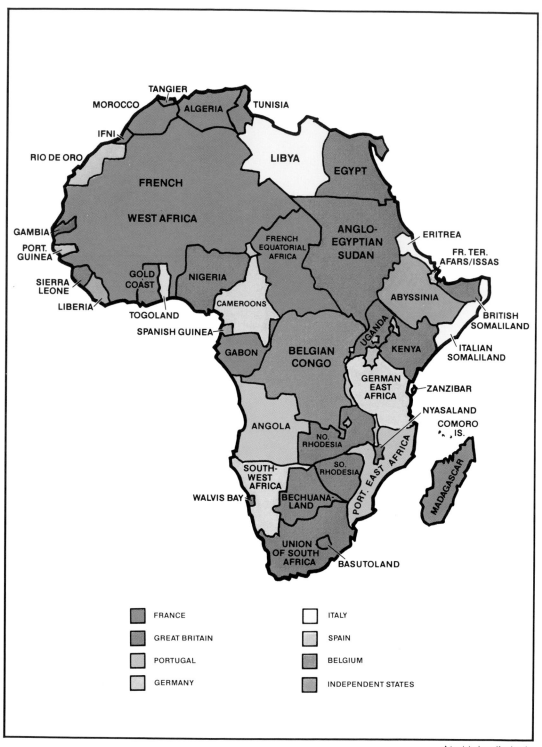

TANGIER
MOROCCO
ALGERIA
TUNISIA
IFNI
RIO DE ORO
LIBYA
EGYPT
FRENCH
WEST AFRICA
GAMBIA
PORT.
GUINEA
FRENCH
EQUATORIAL
AFRICA
ANGLO-
EGYPTIAN
SUDAN
ERITREA
FR. TER.
AFARS/ISSAS
SIERRA
LEONE
LIBERIA
GOLD
COAST
NIGERIA
ABYSSINIA
BRITISH
SOMALILAND
TOGOLAND
CAMEROONS
SPANISH GUINEA
UGANDA
KENYA
ITALIAN
SOMALILAND
GABON
BELGIAN
CONGO
GERMAN
EAST
AFRICA
ZANZIBAR
ANGOLA
NO.
RHODESIA
NYASALAND
COMORO
IS.
PORT. EAST AFRICA
MADAGASCAR
SOUTH-
WEST
AFRICA
SO.
RHODESIA
WALVIS BAY
BECHUANA-
LAND
UNION
OF SOUTH
AFRICA
BASUTOLAND

FRANCE
GREAT BRITAIN
PORTUGAL
GERMANY
ITALY
SPAIN
BELGIUM
INDEPENDENT STATES

Artwork by Larry Kaushansky

In 1910, after the defeat of the Boers in the Anglo-Boer War, four territories in southern Africa — Cape Colony, Natal, the Transvaal, and the Orange Free State — joined together to form the Union of South Africa within the British Empire. (Colonial map information taken from *The Anchor Atlas of World History,* 1978.)

Limpopo River—came under British rule according to the provisions of the Treaty of Vereeniging. From this point onward, the Boers were called Afrikaners.

The British realized that the Afrikaners would not give up the desire for their own nation. The best idea, the British concluded, was to rule South Africa with the cooperation of the Afrikaners. Therefore, the Cape Colony, Natal, the Orange Free State, and the Transvaal were granted self-government within the British Empire. These four territories joined together to form the Union of South Africa in 1910. The first prime minister of the union was Louis Botha, who had been a Boer general in the Anglo-Boer War.

The Twentieth Century

Tension between the British and the Afrikaners persisted through much of the early twentieth century. In World War I, many Afrikaners supported the Germans against Britain and strongly disagreed with the Botha government's demand that Afrikaner troops seize the German colony of South-West Africa. Despite its reluctance to attack the German-held region, the Union of South Africa became a charter member of the League of Nations and was assigned South-West Africa to administer as a territory.

Labor strikes in the 1920s caused the prime minister, Jan Christian Smuts (who succeeded Botha in 1919), to lose control of the government. A new prime minister, J. B. M. Hertzog—another former Boer general—took over. This government spearheaded the nationalization of a few important industries and lessened the domination of the English-speaking population over the government's economic affairs. It also protected white workers' rights and extended the voting franchise to white women.

The coat of arms of the Union of South Africa featured symbols of the four provinces. The figure of Hope *(top left of shield)* stood for Cape Province; two black wildebeests represented Natal; an orange tree symbolized the Orange Free State; and an ox wagon signified the Transvaal. A springbok *(left)* and a gemsbok *(right)* supported the shield. The translation of the Latin motto is "Union Makes Strength." The Republic of South Africa retained the coat of arms upon independence in 1961.

Courtesy of Embassy of South Africa

The first cabinet of the Union of South Africa included its first three prime ministers: Louis Botha *(bottom row, center)*, Jan Christian Smuts *(top row, far left)*, and J. B. M. Hertzog *(top row, second from right)*.

With the enactment of the government's policy of apartheid, many black workers were forced to work in the mines to support their families.

Elections in 1934 were won by the Unionist party, a merger of the conservative National party (led by Hertzog) and the more liberal South African party (headed by Smuts). The new government passed laws that prohibited blacks from owning land, except within reserved areas that the government had allocated to them. In addition, at this time the Union of South Africa became independent within the British Empire. At the outbreak of World War II in 1939, South Africa was still largely unwilling to participate on the side of Great Britain, although the nation finally declared war against Germany.

The reorganized National party regained sole power in 1948 and the new prime minister, Daniel F. Malan, introduced the policy of apartheid, which has ensured white dominance in South Africa's social, economic, and political affairs ever since. In 1960 the white population voted in favor of complete independence from Great Britain; the Republic of South Africa was proclaimed in 1961.

White Response to Labor Problems

After the Anglo-Boer War, Britain might have granted blacks more rights. But the British government agreed to postpone the question about the status of nonwhites until after whites had achieved self-government. This left the fate of blacks, Coloureds, and Asians in the hands of South Africa's whites.

White politicians faced several problems. First, the number of poor Afrikaners was growing. Second, the mine and factory owners demanded cheaper labor, by which they meant black labor. Politicians thus faced the contradictory demands of British industrialists for cheaper labor, and of other whites, mostly Afrikaners, for higher incomes.

One early response to the labor problem had been to encourage immigration from India. More than 30,000 Indians—including the later Indian leader Mohandas K. Gandhi—came to South Africa in the late nineteenth century and settled mostly in Natal. A different solution to the labor problem was the Natives Land Act of 1913, which, after some modifications, left blacks with access to only 13 percent of the land. This act removed the opportunities for blacks to compete with white farmers, and drove many black farmers off their lands and into the mines and factories.

Courtesy of IDAF

Restrictions on the kinds of jobs blacks could hold became part of the apartheid system. Here, white workers rally in support of the Colour Bar Law.

As a result of the apartheid laws, whole African communities were moved. The old villages might have included fairly fertile lands, with a cluster of round, thatched dwellings *(left)*. The homelands to which the African villagers were sent usually had poorer soil, making gardening difficult and less productive *(below)*.

In 1922 a white workers' strike to protest the hiring of low-paid black workers was brutally suppressed. This event, however, caused the government to pass a Colour Bar Law, reserving skilled, higher-paying jobs for whites. By putting restrictions on black labor, the government solved the problem of white poverty.

Development and Expansion of the Apartheid Policy

South Africa's ongoing industrialization brought more blacks into cities, and white fears of black influence increased. After the 1948 elections, the National party extended apartheid into all areas of life. Education, public accommodations (including

park benches and water fountains), and housing were strictly segregated. Blacks were required to carry passes to certify their right to be in a given area. It became a crime for people of different races to marry or to have sexual relations. Severe laws prohibited protests against these conditions, thus dramatically limiting civil rights for whites as well as for blacks.

The organized black response to these measures began in 1912, when the African National Congress (ANC) was founded. Until the early 1950s, the ANC's tactics involved peaceful protest and pleas to the government to restore their rights. By the late 1950s, however, under the influence of Nelson Mandela and others, the ANC adopted more vigorous tactics, including strikes, marches, and boycotts.

The response of the government was drastic. In 1960, 69 blacks who were protesting the pass laws were killed by members of the South African police force.

Courtesy of IDAF

Supporters of the African National Congress (ANC) carry posters announcing their goals in 1955.

Courtesy of IDAF

Nelson Mandela was a central figure of the ANC in the 1950s. Here, he addresses the All-In Africa Conference at Pietermaritzburg, South Africa, in 1961. In 1964 Mandela was sentenced to life imprisonment, a term he continued to serve in 1989.

Courtesy of American Lutheran Church

In 1976 uprisings occurred in Soweto, the township outside of Johannesburg. Hector Peterson, age 13, was the first person to die in the riots.

In the hot, dry season from November until February, water is scarce in the homelands. People line up at faucets or at visiting government trucks to obtain water needed for cooking and drinking.

Photo by Nancy Durrell McKenna

This beach is reserved for white swimmers and sunbathers, but restrictions on sports facilities also affect Coloured and Asian populations in South Africa.

The ANC and other anti-apartheid organizations were outlawed, and the ANC turned to sabotage to try to force change. Captured in 1962, Mandela was sentenced to life imprisonment in 1964. In 1976 about 500 black students were killed, and since then a number of other black and white protesters have been tortured and have died while in police custody. The most prominent of these activists to die were the black student leader Steve Biko and the white trade unionist Neil Aggett. In the 1980s several thousand more blacks died in anti-apartheid riots.

Coloureds, Asians, and Apartheid

Apartheid also discriminates against Coloureds and Asians, although their positions are somewhat better than the position of blacks. No attempt has been made to settle Asians or Coloureds in homelands, but their living areas are strictly segregated from those of whites. Until 1956 Coloureds in Cape Province had the same voting rights as whites. After 1956 Coloureds could elect four white persons to represent them in Parliament. Late in the 1960s that right also was removed. Asians had similar rights but also suffered from discrimination. They could, however, purchase land in Natal until 1946, when the government

prohibited this practice. The Constitution of 1983 gave each group some political representation.

Although there are deep divisions within the Coloured and Asian populations, each seems generally to oppose apartheid, and some have allied themselves with the blacks. Many Coloureds and Asians are torn between the desire to press for an end to apartheid and the need to protect the rights they now have.

The Issue of Namibia

South Africa has imposed a system in Namibia very similar to apartheid, in which whites—composing about 15 percent of the population—are given access to 44 percent of the land. On this land lies most of Namibia's great mineral wealth, which includes diamonds, copper, lead, and zinc. Blacks are strictly segregated. African areas, for example, must be at least 500 yards from white towns.

In 1966 the United Nations ended South Africa's legal protection of the region, but South Africa remained in control of the country. Since then, an armed resistance movement—the South West African People's Organization (SWAPO)—has carried on guerrilla warfare against South African rule. In addition to its mineral

35

wealth, Namibia has a strategic position—south of Angola, whose Communist government South Africa hopes to overthrow.

According to agreements reached in late 1988, the South African government may allow national elections to take place in Namibia. The plan calls for Namibia's elections to be linked to the withdrawal of Cuban troops who support the Angolan government against South Africa's forces.

The Modern Era

During the 1980s, the National government under State President Pieter Willem Botha maintained its policy of white domination. States of emergency—under which strong limitations on the rights of all ethnic communities could be enacted—were frequently declared. The government has announced that apartheid is an outdated concept, and some reforms have occurred. For example, segregation of some public accommodations has been stopped, and the pass laws have been ended. Furthermore, it is no longer illegal for blacks and whites to marry. But the basic features—black poverty, total denial of black political rights, and land and housing restrictions on blacks—remain.

The Nationals' victory in the elections of 1987 was interpreted as a gesture of approval for the party's program of very gradual modification of apartheid. Elections held in October 1988, however, appeared to tell a different story.

Amid a tense campaign atmosphere, the National party again confirmed its strong majority in the legislative assembly. But the Conservative party—whose political platform supports more-rigid apartheid policies—gained the largest increase of legislative seats. The liberal Progressive Federal party lost seats. These gains and losses suggest that white voters have a variety of reactions to the government's policy of reform.

A further indication of varied opinions within the white community occurred in

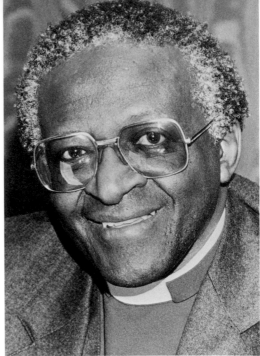

Courtesy of Nobel Foundation

Archbishop Desmond Tutu, head of the Anglican Church in South Africa and the surrounding countries, has taken a strong stance against apartheid. For his efforts, the Nobel Foundation awarded him the Nobel Prize for peace in 1984.

early 1988, when 40 liberal Afrikaners traveled to Dakar, Senegal, to visit with leaders of the ANC. The government, which has outlawed the ANC, regarded the visit as a violation of South African laws.

Government

South Africa became an independent republic on May 31, 1961. For 50 years before that, it had been a union of four provinces within the British Commonwealth. The republic is unusual in that it has three capitals—Cape Town is the legislative capital; Pretoria contains the executive branch; and Bloemfontein hosts the appeals division of the supreme court.

In 1983 whites approved a new and controversial constitution that gives some political influence to Coloureds and Asians but that still denies the participation of blacks. A very small percentage of Coloureds and Asians voted in the first election in which they could choose representatives to Parliament.

STATE PRESIDENT

In 1983 the position of state president, at one time only ceremonial, gained great executive power. The person in this position calls elections, dissolves Parliament, appoints and removes civil servants, declares states of emergency, controls the flow of legislation to Parliament, and vetoes legislation. Chosen by an electoral committee composed of 50 white, 25 Coloured, and 13 Asian representatives from Parliament, the president serves a five-year term.

Cabinet members are appointed by the state president. In 1985 there were 17 ministers, one of whom was Coloured and one of whom was Asian. Each member administers one or more departments.

PARLIAMENT

Legislative power is vested in a tricameral (three-house) Parliament, which is divided into houses for whites, Coloureds, and Asians. The assembly represents whites and has 178 seats. The house of rep-resentatives has 85 members and is set aside for Coloureds. The 45-seat house of delegates represents Asians. Elections are normally held every five years.

The state president determines whether legislation involves what the government terms general affairs or own affairs. General affairs, as the name implies, are important to all three represented population groups and are decided by all three houses. Own affairs, on the other hand, involve only one of the three groups and are debated exclusively in the appropriate house. Affairs involving blacks are entirely under the jurisdiction of the state president.

If the three houses come to different conclusions about a general affair, the question is referred to the President's Council. This body has 60 members, of which 25 are appointed by the state president. Twenty are elected by majority vote in the white assembly, 10 by Coloureds, and 5 by Asians. The decision of the President's Council is final.

State President Pieter Willem Botha (at lectern, center) **delivers his opening address at a joint sitting of the three houses of Parliament in 1984.**

Committees on the President's Council handle conflicts between South Africa's parliamentary houses on matters of general interest.

COURTS

The supreme court has divisions in all four provinces. Its justices are appointed by the state president and can be removed by an act of Parliament. The supreme court is exclusively an appeals court, which means that it reviews the decisions of other courts. Criminal and civil cases originate in a variety of district and magistrates' courts.

Adopted in 1927, the flag of the Republic of South Africa is based on the colors used by the Dutch royal house. In the center of the white stripe, flags represent the two former British colonies of Natal and Cape Colony and the two independent Boer nations: the Orange Free State and the Transvaal.

Over 10,000 runners started the Comrades Marathon from Durban City Hall in 1985. Both blacks and whites can enter the race, which commemorates South African war heroes.

3) The People

In 1989 the population of South Africa was over 35 million. No single way of life exists in South Africa. Rather, many different ways of life, with highly varied customs and characteristics, flourish separately. At one cultural extreme are whites, who live in a modern, technological society. At the other extreme are the San, some of whom live a lifestyle reminiscent of the Stone Age.

About four-fifths of South Africa's population is described as nonwhite. Classified into three groups—blacks, Coloureds, and Asians—each is governed by a separate set of laws. In fact, however, none of the four groups can be described as purely of a single ethnic heritage. According to official 1986 sources, for example, 9 whites petitioned to become Coloureds, 506 Coloureds became whites, 40 Coloureds became blacks, and 666 blacks became Coloureds.

Whites

The majority of white South Africans are descended from people who came from the Netherlands and Great Britain. The first Dutch settlers mixed with German and French Protestant refugees from the European wars of the seventeenth century to form a group once called Boers and now known as Afrikaners. As an entity, whites are called Europeans, but about 60 percent of them are Afrikaners.

Solidly religious and nationalistic, Afrikaners hold most government positions and control the agricultural sector. English-speaking whites, on the other hand, are viewed as more worldly and less rigid in their political opinions. These whites dominate the nation's businesses and industries.

Each white group attends its own churches and community functions and lives in separate areas of the cities. Nevertheless, most South African whites reside in urban areas and enjoy a high standard of living. Splendid suburbs around Johannesburg, Cape Town, Pretoria, and Durban house the wealthiest whites, but even in a middle-income family, the level of comfort is quite high.

Blacks

The 19.5 million blacks, also called Africans, are divided into ethnic groups, or tribes, which are officially known as nationalities. The main ethnic groups include the Zulu, Sotho, Xhosa, Pondo, and other Bantu-speaking peoples.

About four million blacks live on farms owned by whites. An equal number live on tracts of land, called homelands, that the government has set aside for them. The South African government considers blacks to be permanent residents of these homelands. Many blacks travel from the homelands in search of work, principally because the areas' poor soil and lack of jobs prevent the residents from making enough money to sustain their families.

The remainder of the black population lives in townships that surround South Africa's cities. The townships are on land set aside for whites, which means that black residents of townships cannot own their homes but must rent them. These areas created by the white government are, in effect, huge ghettos where resentment against apartheid is strong. Since 1976, several hundred people have died in riots in numerous townships. Soweto, outside Johannesburg, has been the most rebellious.

Courtesy of American Lutheran Church

African ethnic groups make up over two-thirds of South Africa's population.

Courtesy of SATOUR

Some members of the Ndebele, a Bantu-speaking people, artfully paint the walls of their homes. Few Ndebele continue to live in this traditional way, however.

Several kraals, or round-shaped dwellings, form a village in KwaZulu, the homeland organized by the government for the Zulu.

In rural areas most blacks live much as they did before Europeans came to the country—in clusters of traditional dwellings, called kraals. A twentieth-century difference, however, is that many of the African men are away for long periods of time, working in factories or in mines. Cattle are the most-prized possession of the Africans, although certain consumer items that they can afford, like transistor radios, are also popular.

Traditional African homes usually are made of dirt or of grass and straw and often look like cone-shaped beehives. Some dwellings in the homelands are mere corrugated iron boxes or shanties. Several ethnic groups decorate the walls of their houses with vivid paintings, and their traditional dress is often elaborate, consisting of blankets and skins adorned with bright beads and ornaments. Few blacks dress this way today, however. Most are

A woman does her family's laundry in a township outside a large city.

41

urbanized and have adopted European styles of clothing and diet, although their living standards are quite low.

As for the San, they continue to be a nomadic people who engage in hunting and gathering. Some of them live in remote parts of Botswana and Namibia.

Coloureds and Asians

The 2.6 million Coloureds are the mixed-blood descendants of the Khoikhoi and other peoples, including Asian and black slaves, who mingled with the first European settlers. About 77 percent are city dwellers. Largely Afrikaans-speaking, the Coloureds historically have identified themselves with the white population. In recent times, however, some Coloureds have sympathized strongly with the plight of blacks. They have shown their support by petitioning to reclassify themselves as blacks and by joining anti-apartheid groups.

This woman is a member of the South African population classified by the government as Coloured, meaning of mixed ancestry. The group is descended from intermarriages between the country's early European settlers and people of ethnic communities such as the San, the Khoikhoi, and the Asians.

In the Cape Town area, a few thousand Malays—whose ancestors were brought by the Dutch from southeast Asia during the colonial period—still form a distinct community. Most of the other 800,000 Asians are descendants of workers brought from India in the 1860s to work on sugar plantations and are found chiefly in Natal province.

Views of Apartheid

Racial discrimination did not start with apartheid. Apartheid is simply a more systematic, all-encompassing program that deeply influences all aspects of South Africa's social, political, economic, and cultural relations.

At its height, apartheid consisted of four categories of laws. The first reserved

At an outdoor market in Cape Town, a woman who is part of the group known as the Cape Malays examines a potential purchase.

Supporters of apartheid hold that much of South Africa's industrial and technological development – represented by the computerized control board of a gasification plant – has been the result of white influence.

skilled jobs, access to good land, and other economic benefits only for white people. The second gave political rights and power only to whites. The third law instituted strict segregation of living areas and social relations. The final law created 10 black-only areas, called homelands, out of the 13 percent of the land reserved for blacks.

THE PRO-APARTHEID VIEW

The National party—particularly its leader from 1959 to 1966, Prime Minister Hendrik Verwoerd—presented apartheid as the solution to South Africa's cultural and ethnic complexity. The government usually defined this complexity as a clash between competing nationalisms. The white nation, the Nationals argued, was fully developed, while the cultures of Coloureds, Asians, and blacks were not. Whites, therefore, needed total political power to keep order and to preserve the state. Most whites also equate black nationalism with Communism, against which they see apartheid as a defense.

This policy, which has also been called separate development, in theory would allow blacks to prosper along their own lines in the homelands. Thus separated, the various competing nationalisms could avoid clashes, and stability would be preserved. Whites point to the instability in some black African nations as an example of what might happen if apartheid is not maintained.

Another justification often given for apartheid is that South Africa's prosperity is due largely to the activity of whites. This group needs to protect its accomplishments from what it believes would be destruction if the country were in black hands. Finally, supporters of apartheid often argue that if blacks come to power they will discriminate against whites, who have no other place to go.

THE ANTI-APARTHEID VIEW

Primary to the argument of those who oppose apartheid is the concern that the amount of land set aside for blacks is far too small to ever support those who are to

43

Courtesy of SATOUR

Critics of apartheid charge that one of its aims is to preserve a large, cheap labor force, especially for dangerous jobs—such as underground mining—that other workers refuse to do.

live on it. In addition, the black-reserved lands contain too few significant natural resources, are burdened by poor soil, and have very little industry. Thus, those blacks who now reside in the homelands live in poverty.

These facts have led critics to charge that the real purpose of apartheid is to preserve white supremacy and a cheap supply of black labor. Unable to find work in the homelands, millions of blacks actually live in white areas of the country and work as laborers in mines and factories and as servants in white people's residences. This is the case for over half of the 4.5 million Xhosa people, who, until recently, were theoretically citizens of the homeland of Transkei.

An important feature of apartheid is the low earning power of blacks. All wage rates vary greatly. Blacks earn about one-fourth as much as whites in the insurance business and about one-tenth as much as whites in the coal mining industry. According to various calculations, many Africans earn too little to sustain life.

Many critics also argue that apartheid violates human rights, which most people of the West regard as belonging to all people. The South African system denies blacks any significant influence in managing their own affairs.

Another criticism of apartheid is that the government's homelands scheme artificially subdivides blacks. Nearly a century of urbanization has reduced many of the ethnic differences between blacks, and government policies have tried forcibly to reestablish them.

Apartheid has brought world condemnation upon South Africa. For example, the country has been expelled from the United Nations, and many Western and African countries have imposed economic sanctions, which prohibit various kinds of business dealings.

Language

In South Africa each ethnic group has its own language. Afrikaans—one of the two official languages (English is the other)—

44

is derived from the Dutch spoken by seventeenth-century colonists. It also includes words and phrases from various African languages, as well as from Malay, Portuguese, English, French, and German.

Coloureds speak Afrikaans, but those living in Cape Town tend to speak English also. Asians speak English as well as their own languages, which include Tamil, Gujarati, Hindi, and Chinese. When talking among themselves, blacks use their own languages, such as Xhosa, Zulu, Tswana, and Swazi.

Blacks also learn the language of their employers or an all-purpose Creole language called Fanagalo—a combination of Zulu and English. Since most of the education for blacks before 1953 was through mission schools, the 40 percent of blacks who received primary education tended to learn English in addition to their own languages. Afrikaans is now also obligatory in all South African schools.

Literature

Afrikaans, spoken by about 60 percent of the white population, was scorned for a long time as a written medium. In 1925, however, it was finally recognized as an official language. Courses in a number of universities in other countries now teach it. More than 10,000 books have been published in Afrikaans, which has been distinct from Dutch for less than 200 years.

There are a number of significant Afrikaner authors. Andre P. Brink, who also teaches literature at Rhodes University in Grahamstown, has written novels, such as *A Dry White Season*, that criticize apartheid. Many of the plays of Athol Fugard have drawn praise around the world. *Boesman and Lena* and *Master Harold and the Boys* are among them. In order to reach a larger audience, these Afrikaner authors write primarily in English.

A few white, English-speaking authors have achieved world renown. The late Alan Paton, author of *Cry, the Beloved Country,* was famous for several decades. More recently Nadine Gordimer has achieved critical acclaim for novels like *Burger's Daughter* and *July's People,* which attack apartheid. The latter story speculates about life in South Africa after a black revolution.

Missionaries have done much to develop African literature in South Africa. Before 1920 Bantu-speaking Africans were virtually illiterate, and their literature developed slowly. Pioneer work was done by such writers as Thomas Mofolo, Solomon Plaatje, and R. R. Dhlomo. *Wrath of the Ancestors,* a play by Archibald C. Jordan, is the best-known work in Xhosa and exemplifies the modern tendency to explore themes associated with urban life.

Censorship has become an increasingly significant issue in South Africa. The country has 170 newspapers, many publishing

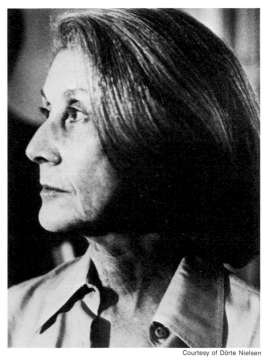

Courtesy of Dörte Nielsen

Nadine Gordimer, author of novels such as *A Sport of Nature* and *Burger's Daughter,* has become an effective voice in the anti-apartheid campaign.

firms, and several radio networks. All of these media, but especially the newspapers, are strictly controlled by the government.

Education and Religion

South Africa's official education policy discriminates against nonwhites. Whites are allotted 1.5 times more funds than Asians, 2.4 times more than Coloureds, and 12 times more than blacks. Indeed, until 1981 schooling was not compulsory for black children.

The law requires all white children between the ages of 7 and 16 to attend school. White and Coloured children go to free elementary and secondary schools, which are financed by the national and provincial governments. South Africa has about 7,000 free schools for the exclusive use of black children. In the 1980s more than 20 percent of South Africa's black children attended classes. South Africa also operates several universities and colleges that serve the varied ethnic groups, although some of the white institutions admit blacks.

Photo by Nancy Durrell McKenna

Educational facilities are not equal for all South African children. Schools for blacks are usually crowded, with a greater student-to-teacher ratio.

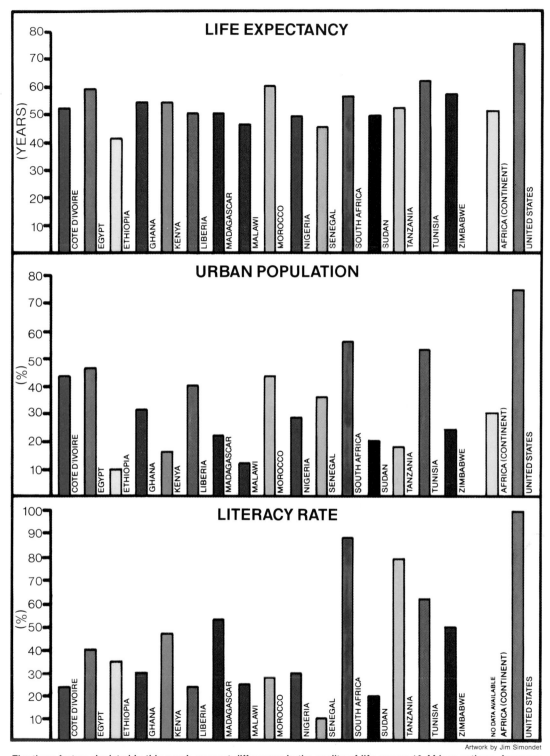

Artwork by Jim Simondet

The three factors depicted in this graph suggest differences in the quality of life among 16 African nations. Averages for the United States and the entire continent of Africa are included for comparison. Data taken from "1987 World Population Data Sheet" and *PC-Globe.*

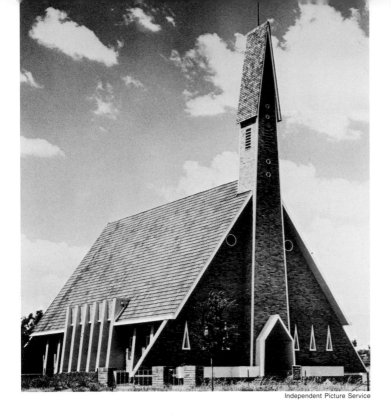

Most Afrikaners and Coloureds are members of the Dutch Reformed Church, which has its origins in Dutch Protestantism.

The literacy rate for the various ethnic groups has been estimated to be 98 percent for whites, 85 percent for Asians, 75 percent for Coloureds, and 50 percent for blacks. Even the lowest of these figures, however, is higher than the statistics in some other areas of Africa.

More than half of the white South Africans, including almost all the Afrikaans-speakers, belong to the Dutch Reformed Church. In recent years, however, varying views of apartheid—some strongly opposed to each other—have led to splits within the church. The next largest denomination is Anglican, which is supported by nearly 16 percent of the whites. Eight percent of the white population is Methodist, 5 percent is Roman Catholic, 4 percent is Presbyterian, and approximately 4 percent is Jewish.

Most Coloureds are members of either the Dutch Reformed or Anglican churches, though the Malays of Cape Town are Muslim—followers of the Islamic religion. The Asians have retained their own faiths, mainly Hinduism and Islam. Many blacks are animists—that is, they believe that all things, both living and nonliving, possess a vital, natural life force. Christians are divided not only among European denominations but also among roughly 2,000 African sects. About 80 percent of these sects have been given government recognition. Many of the African churches combine traditional African beliefs with Christian doctrines.

Health

In South Africa health statistics are better for whites than they are for any other group in the country. Easy access to quality medical facilities and a more nutritious diet contribute to the generally good health whites enjoy. Indeed, the most common causes of death among whites in South Africa—heart disease, stroke, and cancer—are the same as those for whites in Europe and North America. In the 1980s life expectancy for whites was about 70 years, and the infant mortality figure was 15 deaths in every 1,000 live births. Both statistics are similar to those in industrialized nations of the West.

In contrast, health conditions for blacks, Coloureds, and Asians are worse. For many people in the nonwhite groups, poor health can be directly related to inadequate diet. Low incomes and the continued reliance on traditional foods—which often are nutritionally deficient—have made it difficult for these groups to receive basic food requirements. In addition, many of the townships in which blacks live lack proper sewers and safe drinking water—conditions that add to the risk of disease. Tuberculosis, malaria, measles, and diphtheria —all treatable ailments—claim large numbers of blacks. Although excellent private medical facilities exist in urban areas, few nonwhite groups can afford them.

In 1987 South Africa's health minister told Parliament about the nation's problem with AIDS (acquired immune deficiency syndrome). Nearly equal numbers of whites (1,140) and blacks (1,093) were reported to be carrying the virus. Many of

Courtesy of American Lutheran Church

Pottery making—using imaginative designs and varied shapes—is an important African art form.

Courtesy of American Lutheran Church

Health statistics for blacks in South Africa are worse than for any other ethnic community in the country. A black child can expect to live to the age of 55.

the black South Africans who had tested positively worked under contract in the mines.

The current life expectancy figure for blacks is 55 years; for Coloureds, 59 years; and for Asians, 66 years. Infant mortality rates for nonwhites also are worse than those for whites. Indeed, the rate for blacks is more than 10 times greater than it is for whites. In the 1980s, 200 black babies, 81 Coloured babies, and 25 Asian babies died out of every 1,000 infants born in those groups. Africa as a whole averages 113 deaths per 1,000 live births.

Art and Music

Hugo Naudé, J. H. Pierneef, and R. Gwelo Goodman are some of the South African artists who have broken with the traditional style of painting that specializes in romantic landscapes. This modern school has begun a new era in South African painting, and artists like Jean Welz, Alexis Preller, and Walter Battis excel in the new form. South Africa also has produced important works of art in mosaic, tapestry, handmade jewelry, and the graphic arts.

Traditional African arts have their roots in prehistory. Some of the most interesting examples of this ancient art form are paintings on the walls of caves that are found from Zimbabwe to the Cape. Carved wooden sculptures and beautiful woven cloths are also among age-old African art forms.

White South African composers, such as John Joubert, Arnold van Wyk, and Hubert Du Plessis, contribute to the international classical style. The republic's rich store of folk songs, called *Boeremusiek* (folk music), has achieved great popularity among whites both inside and outside the country.

African peoples in South Africa have a rich and ancient tradition of dance and music. The music is either sung or played on instruments such as drums, reed pipes, xylophones, and other percussion instruments. A number of blacks—notably the Xhosa jazz singer Miriam Makeba and the trumpet player Hugh Masekela—have achieved international recognition as musical performers. Both are now in exile from South Africa.

Food

The oldest and most typical fare on white South African tables combines the recipes the colonists brought from Europe and the rich spice and curry dishes of the Malays. Bobotie, kabobs, and *blatjang* (chutney)—the latter made from tropical fruits, such as mangoes and guavas—are local adaptations of the foods from both the East and the West. The curries and peppers made by East Indians—who came in the late nineteenth century to work on the Natal sugarcane plantations—also became popular. These dishes were altered by the addition

Courtesy of R. L. Watson

The sound of drums and xylophones form the background rhythm of much of South Africa's traditional ethnic music.

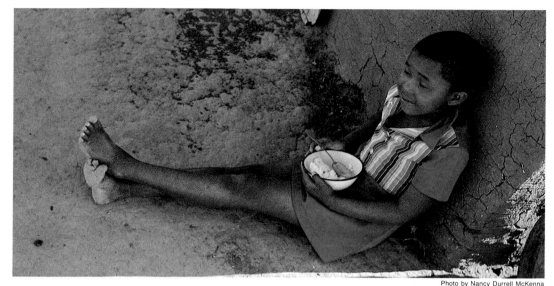

A young Zulu eats cornmeal mush, called mealies, before leaving for school. In the Zulu language, the dish is named *iphalishi.*

of fruits grown in South Africa, such as pineapples and limes.

Biltong (a dried meat akin to jerky) is a South African staple that evolved from the early necessity of having a nourishing food that would not spoil during long treks. The diet of most black South Africans is simple. The main food is maize (corn), which the blacks call mealies and which they usually eat as porridge.

Fresh seafood often appears on the dinner tables of white South Africans.

Sports

The climate of South Africa is ideally suited to many forms of outdoor recreation, ranging from rugby to mountaineering and from deep-sea fishing to hunting in the lowlands of the Transvaal. White South Africans are avid sports enthusiasts and have won international acclaim in many different activities. Gary Player and Sally Little are well-known South African golfers. Tennis players such as Cliff Drysdale, Kevin Curran, and Johan Kriek also have been successful. The principal winter game is rugby, and cricket is the most popular summer sport.

Blacks have also come to enjoy European sports, some of which—like soccer and track—are partially integrated. Black athletes, however, suffer from lack of training facilities, money, and leisure time. Many international sporting competitions,

Courtesy of American Lutheran Church

Near Durban, black swimmers enjoy the coastal waters on beaches set aside by the government for black South Africans.

including the Olympics, boycott South Africa. This action has driven many black and white athletes, such as the distance runners Sidney Maree and Zola Budd, into exile.

Courtesy of SATOUR

Rugby, a field sport that originated in Great Britain in the 1800s, is played throughout South Africa.

In Cape Province, farm workers load bundles of freshly picked fruit into crates.

4) The Economy

Until the end of the nineteenth century, South Africa was almost a completely agricultural country, with both Afrikaners and blacks cultivating crops and raising livestock to feed their families. With the discovery of gold and diamonds, however, the need for investment in mining complexes and machinery propelled South Africa into the industrial age.

In the first 50 years of the twentieth century, the country produced more than half of the world's gold. The sale of its gold enabled South Africa to import many goods, in some cases giving the white population a standard of living greater than that of Canada or the United States.

With adequate iron ore and wealth from the richest supply of gold on the African continent, South Africa was able to establish major iron and steel industries. After World War II it began to develop other industries, and since then South Africa's net national income has increased as the price of gold and other minerals has risen. In the 1980s agriculture, forestry, and fishing accounted for 12 percent of the total output of goods. Mining made up 13 percent, private manufacturing and construction produced 25 percent, and trade accounted for 12 percent.

Agriculture

South Africa's major agricultural problems are soil erosion and low rainfall levels. Only about 17 percent of the total area of

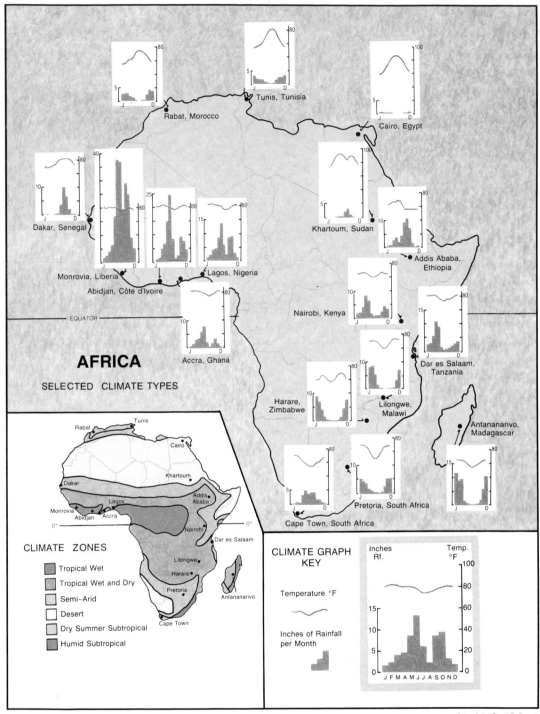

AFRICA

SELECTED CLIMATE TYPES

Rabat, Morocco

Tunis, Tunisia

Cairo, Egypt

Dakar, Senegal

Khartoum, Sudan

Addis Ababa, Ethiopia

Monrovia, Liberia

Lagos, Nigeria

Abidjan, Côte d'Ivoire

Nairobi, Kenya

Dar es Salaam, Tanzania

EQUATOR

Accra, Ghana

Harare, Zimbabwe

Lilongwe, Malawi

Antananarivo, Madagascar

Pretoria, South Africa

Cape Town, South Africa

CLIMATE ZONES

- Tropical Wet
- Tropical Wet and Dry
- Semi-Arid
- Desert
- Dry Summer Subtropical
- Humid Subtropical

Rabat
Tunis
Cairo
Dakar
Khartoum
Addis Ababa
Lagos
Monrovia
Abidjan Accra
Nairobi
Dar es Salaam
Lilongwe
Harare
Pretoria
Antananarivo
Cape Town

CLIMATE GRAPH KEY

Inches Rf.
Temp. °F

Temperature °F

Inches of Rainfall per Month

J F M A M J J A S O N D

Artwork by Carol F. Barrett

These climate graphs show the monthly changes in the average rainfall received and in the average temperature from January to December for the capital cities of 16 African nations. The data for Cape Town generally is representative of the drier western half of the country, and a seaside location moderates the city's temperatures. Pretoria, on the other hand, is on the edge of the more humid eastern region and, unlike Cape Town, receives most of its rainfall during the Southern Hemisphere's summer months (December and January). The city's summer temperatures are relatively cool because of its location in the highlands. Data taken from *World-Climates* by Willy Rudloff, Stuttgart, 1981.

54

the republic is suitable for cultivation, and only about 11 percent is highly fertile. Flash floods and rain runoff sometimes destroy even these fertile areas. The impact of soil erosion is most noticeable in the homelands because of dense population, overgrazing by livestock, and generally inefficient farming methods.

Maize is the most valuable crop of South Africa, as well as the staple food of the black population. Only about one-tenth of the total maize crop, however, is raised within the homelands. Wheat is plentiful and is grown chiefly in the southwestern Cape, which is the winter rainfall area of the country. Oats, rye, barley, and sorghum (a cereal grain) are grown to a lesser extent.

Fruit is second to maize in production, and much of it is exported in cold storage or in bottled or canned form. Although no

Courtesy of SATOUR

Grapes are harvested in the wine-making area located 150 miles from Cape Town.

Courtesy of Embassy of South Africa

By standing on tall ladders, laborers are able to pick the ripest fruits from a grove of orange trees. Although no citrus fruits are native to South Africa, they grow well in the country's hot climate.

Workers load stalks of sugarcane—a crop that was introduced in Natal in the nineteenth century—onto carts for processing into granulated sugar.

Long-haired sheep graze on the sparse grasses of the karroos, or plains, of southwestern South Africa.

citrus or temperate-climate fruits are native to South Africa, almost all of them are grown successfully in the republic. Wine making is also an important part of agriculture, with most of the vineyards lying within 150 miles of Cape Town. The coastal districts of Natal and KwaZulu grow sugarcane, which was cultivated widely as early as 1870. Other important field crops are tobacco, peanuts, and vegetables.

The wool produced in South Africa is of high quality. By the end of World War II, South Africa had become the second largest producer of fine wool in the world and the fourth largest wool-exporting country. Dairy products and cattle are also important to the economy, but these are produced mainly for the domestic market.

Because blacks regard livestock as a way to measure wealth, they own large numbers of cattle. Black ranchers resist the efforts of agricultural officers to eliminate the weaker animals in order to thin the herds and thereby to strengthen them. The African nationalist movement has supported the farmers' resistance on the grounds that the problem is not overcrowded herds but too little pastureland. Despite studies that indicate blacks in the homelands have far too little land for successful agriculture, few attempts have been made to solve this problem.

South African gold is often sold in the form of Krugerrands
—coins containing one ounce of the precious metal.

Mining

South Africa's strong economic position is
largely the result of its mineral resources,
particularly gold, of which it is the largest
producer in the world. Despite the twentieth century's economic ups and downs,
South Africa's gold mining industry has
been remarkably prosperous. The Witwatersrand gold mines were supplemented
after World War II by the opening of a
series of rich mines in the Orange Free
State. Production increased steadily and
reached 20 million ounces in 1959. As the
price of gold rose in the 1970s, mining
became even more profitable.

The discovery that uranium could be
produced from mine waste brought addi-
tional revenue to the mining companies.
The first uranium treatment plant was
started in 1951; the seventeenth was com-
pleted in 1957. Twenty-three gold mining
companies produce uranium, which is used
by nuclear power plants to produce energy. The Atomic Energy Board, on behalf
of the state, owns the uranium, most of
which is exported to Great Britain and
other Western nations.

South Africa's sale of diamonds rose
steadily after World War II. South
African diamonds amount to more than
one-sixth of the total sale that goes

A copper mining complex stretches over acres of land at Phalaborwa.

Miners file past a 200-foot-high pile of quartzite near the Daggafontein mines.

Diamonds are a leading item among South African exports.

A worker takes a sample of rough gold, which will be tested to determine its purity.

through the Central Selling Organization, which acts on behalf of South Africa and other producers. South Africa is the world's leading source of gem diamonds. (Two stones from its fields are among the British Crown jewels.) The nation is also a leader—second only to Zaire—in the production of industrial diamonds.

Coal outstrips in value all other mining products, except gold and the minerals used for making nuclear energy. The production of iron ore, though low in total value, enables South Africa to make most of the steel needed for its own use. The republic also produces platinum, copper, asbestos, manganese, and chromium in exportable amounts.

Fishing

South Africa's coastline provides access to both the Atlantic and Indian oceans. As a result, the nation's waters are rich sources of marine life. The Benguela Current, which carries fish northward, cuts through South Africa's western seas. From this coastal movement, South Africa harvests four-fifths of its annual catch.

More than 1,000 varieties of sea life, including mackerel, anchovies, pilchards, hake, herring, and maasbankers, are found off South Africa's coasts. Walvis Bay is one of the nation's principal fishing areas. Much of the catch taken between Walvis Bay and Cape Town is canned, although some is frozen; a small amount of the lobsters caught are exported to the United States, Europe, and Japan.

Manufacturing

The government closely regulates industry to ensure that the interests of the white population are satisfied. Secondary industry, though well established before World War II, grew very quickly in the postwar period. About half of the total value of private industry's output comes from the

Photo by Nancy Durrell McKenna

Construction work, using locally produced building materials, is an important aspect of South Africa's industry.

Transvaal region alone. Metals and engineering are leading areas of manufacturing and are closely followed by consumer goods, such as food, beverages, tobacco, textiles, building materials, and chemicals.

South Africa encourages private enterprise, but the state also participates in industry through the Industrial Development Corporation of South Africa. Major projects have been financed by the corporation to produce oil from coal, to develop phosphate deposits in the Transvaal, and to produce pulp for rayon. A considerable amount of nationalization (government ownership) also exists in South Africa. Railways, ports, telecommunications, airlines, and much of the overland transportation network are operated by the government. The largest steel producer in the country is also a state-run corporation.

The Industrial Development Corporation helps to finance industries on the edges of the homelands. Some overseas business interests have also been allowed to participate in this project. But the homelands attract very little private investment, which further limits their potential for becoming self-sufficient.

South Africa's Work Force

Blacks make up the basic work force throughout South Africa. The mines and the iron and steel industries depend on migratory workers, who are housed in single-sex compounds and who sign 9- to 15-month contracts. Wages are low, but the food and health standards are somewhat better than those found in the homelands. Nevertheless, because underground work in the mines is dangerous and poorly paid, it has been difficult to recruit an adequate number of workers from South Africa itself. As a result, other Africans have been flown in by mine recruiting agencies from Malawi in East Africa, and about one-quarter of the gold miners come from nearby Mozambique.

Other nonwhite groups fill intermediary roles between the unskilled work performed by the Africans and the skilled or professional work done by the whites. For example, in and near Durban, Asians work in secondary industry, keep small shops, run buses, and tend market gardens. Outside the city they provide services in small villages or work the land. Coloureds play a similar role in and around Cape Town,

Independent Picture Service

Stacks of timber tower over black workers in Transkei, one of the independent homelands in southern Africa.

After clashes with security guards at the Matla Colliery, where six protesters were injured, striking miners chant slogans in support of the outlawed ANC in August 1987.

where there are fewer blacks to take agricultural jobs. The white-controlled government is trying to push black workers out of the western areas of Cape Province in order to give jobs to Coloureds.

Whites occupy a privileged place within the economy. A large proportion of the managerial positions were once held by English-speaking whites. Great efforts on the part of the Afrikaner community, however, have increased the number of Afrikaners in these positions. Although many of the white workers do not have advanced skills, they are highly paid. In theory, all skilled jobs are supposed to be held by whites, but in fact the white population is too small to fill all the available jobs. Nonwhites not only occupy over half of the semiskilled jobs, but they also perform a number of skilled jobs, though without the prestige or higher pay that whites enjoy.

Trade Unions

Since the enactment of the 1924 Industrial Conciliation Act, white trade unions have had extensive and well-defined rights. But this law did not recognize black unions, and blacks could not join white trade unions. In 1981, however, certain black unions were legalized and could claim bargaining rights. This move was a major step in providing basic rights to South Africa's workers. Strikes by the blacks were illegal until 1973, when the government passed legislation designed to give many black workers the right to strike.

In August 1987 the black National Union of Mineworkers called the biggest strike in South Africa's history, involving at least 200,000 miners. Central to the complaints of the workers were low wages and poor benefits. Talks between union leaders and officials of the Chamber of Mines, which represents the mine companies, broke down, and clashes erupted. Police fired rubber bullets and tear gas at striking workers, and mine employees who crossed the picket line were harassed by those who answered the strike call. Thousands of striking miners were fired, and dozens of mines were temporarily closed.

61

The miners' strike of 1987 focused on wages and work conditions, including the single-sex mining compounds in which workers live for months at a time, unable to visit their families in the homelands.

The matter ended when the companies agreed to improve benefits but not to raise salaries more than the new contracts stated. Both offers were accepted by the union.

Transportation

Since South Africa has no navigable rivers, internal transport depends on railways, highways, and airlines. Over the years, the nation has developed the best overland transportation network in Africa. Railway construction has expanded steadily since the formation of the Union of South Africa in 1910. Since 1936 national roads have connected the most important cities in the country.

Domestic and international air services are run by South African Airways (SAA), the largest carrier on the African continent. SAA's operations have been hampered in recent years by the refusal of some countries to allow the airline to fly

Many international airlines fly to South Africa's airports.

over them. The overflight ban—a protest against South Africa's apartheid policy—has forced SAA to extend its routes to avoid the prohibited areas.

The Future

In 1986—in response both to the uprisings in South Africa and to anti-apartheid campaigns at home—many African and Western countries imposed economic sanctions on South Africa. These penalties sharply limited investments and trade. Businesses and universities were pressured to withdraw their investments, and many did so. It was hoped that these measures would help persuade South Africa's whites to dismantle apartheid fully, but so far the sanctions have not achieved the desired result.

Many nations support sanctions because they appear to avoid bloodshed while helping the struggle against apartheid. If these measures continue to fail, South Africa's ethnic tensions are likely to intensify. The disunity of such vast potential in people and natural resources would be a global tragedy.

Courtesy of Embassy of South Africa

P. W. Botha became head of the South African government in 1978. Although supportive of both strict law enforcement and an increase in military strength, Botha has advocated some reforms of the apartheid policy. In general, however, apartheid remains in force, in spite of economic sanctions and international pressure.

Courtesy of SATOUR

South Africa has an excellent railway network. Among its main attractions is the Blue Train, a luxury line featuring elaborate cuisine and lush accommodations that few but the wealthy can afford.

Index